The Climax

By Nelly Dreams
    Formally known as
      "Lovechild"

The Climax
Published by
C & C Publishing Company
WASHINGTON, DC 20002

Copyright © 2007 by C & C Publishing Company c/o Chanelle J Flowers

ISBN 13: 978-0-615-19230-7

Printed in the United States

All rights reserved. No part of this book may be reproduced in any form, excerpt for the inclusion of brief quotations in review, without permission in writing from the author/publisher.

For general information and to contact Nelly Dreams, you may email her at dreams2pub@gmail.com.

 C & C Publishing Company

EVERYBODY:
Much love to you all! Thank you for your support and encouraging me to go after my dreams.

TABLE OF EMOTIONS

HEART & SOUL........................7

MIND & BODY......................40

SPECIAL THANKS...................134

UPCOMING WORK; 137

HEART

AND

SOUL

A TRIBUTE TO LOVE

I just touched the clouds
At the kiss of your lips.
I hope to never come down
From this high you've got me on.
I hear angels singing
As we make love in the midst of mid-air.
Just to hold you
Brings much happiness to my soul
And calms my heart.
Acres of Land, Multitudes of Life itself
Can't compare to the way you make me feel.
It's like my dreams…
Aren't really mine unless you're in them;
Oops, not again! I've fallen'!

WE BELONG

*You & I are like apples from a tree
It's hard to come between, you and me
Love is the part that's so different to explain
My heart & soul is what you claim,
You make me feel so brand new
Do question about it, our love is true.
I know this isn't right.
But you're on my mind both day and night.
Dream about you and I happily married,
Living together as one; to think it was supposed to be.
It's very scary to me!
Life without you, I just couldn't take it.
Truly because baby, "We belong."*

SOMEONE LIKE YOU

*Every night I've dreamed to find
Someone like you that would be mine
One day I will bow down; kneel on my knee
To ask you to marry me
Just to hear you say "yes"
Gets me so excited…
Thinking about that special day
We'll vow to everlastin' love
Only you can make me feel
So good to have someone like you!
It must've been heaven sent
A beautiful creature in a very mysterious way
To have and hold; my past is now sold.
Only for you, the key holder of my heart
It was love from the very start
That the Angel of love
Flying like a dove let such a blessing
Glowing like the shadow of the sun
Let me know that you were the one.*

REFLECTION OF THE HEART

One look into your eyes
Gives me joy & I smile
Knowing that you are
My friend and lover
Overwhelmed by the way you touch me
Ever so gently; turns me completely around
Hitting me in the center of my heart,
Showing just how real you love is.
The kisses you place upon my ups
Which ran all threw my body
Let me know that you are the one
For real it's seems but yet still hard to believe
That after all these years, six to be exact
We so happen to find each other
~ So unexpectedly~
Now I can truly say
You are my future & beyond
I can't tell you or anyone else
How this feeling has taken over my heart,
I know that you & I will always be
Together you can't see
It's you that lie in me.

UNCONTROLLABLE LOVE

Butterflies at the sound at your voice
I smile at the at every twinkle in your eye;
A skipped beat from my heat at your kiss- - -
And I exhale
Then say to myself "What is it?"
You turn me into something I wasn't
A female who's into another.
I look around to find only no one like you
That I could make me feel this way;
So forever stay here in my arms,
Cause you calm my soul.
Again I look in the mirror to find Love.

LOVE SPELL

You got me memorized
Hypnotized when I look into your eyes
You spoke, killing my search of someone special
As the hoping & wishing dies.
It's amazing how you've captured my heart!
With one sweet & oh such passionate kiss
Your touch sends me on a soul stirring
Ride, my personal genie might I add
You are my smile when I am sad
The thought of you makes my heart skip
A beat, missing & wanting
Your hugs & kisses start the heat
That sparks in your left and trying to be
What's right in the center of my heart?
Could you be mine, would you be mine?
The spell you put upon me
It's like a fish at the bottom of the sea;
Needing & wanting your company 247
I wish you to be near at all times
Possible such good poison to my soul
I will die trying to live forever
With you, if this is real
Magic and it's in your love.

LOST IN LOVE

I thought your love was no longer,
I thought your love was past-tense;
I thought I wouldn't feel like this anymore.
I saw you and I began to think
"Where did we go wrong?"
I was there for you as you were for me
I still love you can't you see
I kissed your lips and I melted
Like butter, tasting what was mine
Now you say to leave it behind,
You might be playing right!
But that was on my mind all night
I will admit that I do miss you
And your crazy & jealous ways; most of all
Your love got me reminiscing
Thinking about how it would've been.
Now all we have is our
Memories; so lock them up for
Safety from all harm
Is in your love one's arms.

REBIRTH OF OUR LOVE

Just three years ago you became my boo,
For eternity, our love will be.
Laid there in love bliss
Bashfully thinking of everything but the right.
You watched beauty shine so bright,
In the wee-hours of the morning.
My heart, you began owning
At the kiss of your lips;
Sending my soul on a non-ending eclipse.
Wounded for life, we thought
Now look at us
Back together and don't know how.
Just to relive that moment once more,
It's every other season's chore.
To lose the love we shared then,
Only to grow in what's spared.
Come on baby, reminisce with me
And enjoy yourself & live your life.
By loving what we gave birth.

A LIFETIME LOVE

Constant thoughts of you
Lingers on my mind;
I find you to be my hope for tomorrow.
My heart cries happiness,
That its contentment has arrived
So heavily, you got me in love like no other.
You are my friend, companion, and lover
And as the days goes by;
Often feel you are the soul mate that I've searched
for.
I look at you & me and ask myself everyday
"Could she be my wife or is she just someone to love
But all & all, I want to grow old with you"
So what I am thinking and feeling so deeply
I am starring my deal woman in the face
And there's nothing left to do about it.
So baby, walk with me up that aisle
And let's start eternity together.

LOVE'S TAKEN OVER

The first time I saw your sweet and lovely face,
I knew that you were the one
To make all my dreams come true.
Even though, I have always wished
To find someone as beautiful as you;
For my lover and my wife.
I went to bed with you
On my mind like an constant jewel
To wear everyday till eternity.
I never thought I would find love
Ever again in life.
I whisper "I love you"
In the night of loneliness,
Hoping you will hear my desirable cry.
Wanting you near at all times
The thought of you just being a dream
Scared me half to death
I've waited for this precious moment;
That I would love you more than ever before.
It came so quickly and oh so easy
However, I just blushed & smiled
Oh so sweet & oh so heavenly.
I just can't seem to love anyone else
Cause me heart only loves you.
I often daydream and wish
You were here with me
Holding, kissing me, oh so gently
Then we lay and fall fast asleep.

REJECTED LOVE

When you say "I love you"
Do you really mean it?
Or just saying it to get by?
It's murder to the heart
When you give and don't receive
Love in return, believe me
I've been there memories of times.
Life is too short to waste love on love,
So what do you do with all the agony & pain?
After devoting all your trust
Into someone that really doesn't care.
Looking & hoping all your dreams
Will still come to pass,
The last thing on your mind
Is that they don't want you,
Or just playing with your emotions
Like that's going to help any.
So listen up here baby,
I have plenty of reasons
To love myself and you just gave me
The best one of all, you and your rejected love.

MYSTERY OF LOVE

Why love?
When love can be broken;
By the righteousness of life.
Why put your heart in one's hand?
When it can be crushed;
With one untruthful comment.
Why is "I love you" so easy to say?
When it's just said to get what you want;
While hurting one's heart & soul.
Why promise?
When tomorrow is a new day;
Full of different thoughts, hopes & dreams.
Why say "I will always love you?"
If you can't forever show it;
To assure that you are real.
You can't tell me, can you?

SECOND SENSE

A scent,
a soft breeze of yesterday and today.
Beautiful flowers growing in the midst
Of the moments of passion.
I breathe in to grasp every aspect of being loved
Remembering the past and future to come
Blinds me, so overwhelmed by the powers of
Sexuality of a woman to woman
Enlighten my sight to who I am
So I sniff…then I sniff again
And find myself lost in deep thought of you
Umm, the scent of you!

CHANGE ME

If this was spiritually right,
She would've been my wife that night.
I toss those feelings out the door,
Made heaven my home, for sure!
Can't lose what I've built so far,
Beautiful, black as tar.
Change these thoughts to faint memories
Of the past two centuries.
Take this back from me,
Let me breathe please.
Another blessing is waiting near,
So put down that beer.
Cast my burdens upon him,
Restore my faith within.
God, Jesus, Dad; thy three men
By their grace & mercy,
I will make it till the end.

MAKE ME WHOLE AGAIN

Waitin' suspense
Of when I'll next kiss your lips.
Sensual feelings throughout my body
Leaving me, your path of beautiful substance
Magical chemistry above earth's surface
Missin' you desperately
Needin' to combine our souls once more
Before I go crazy;
Facin' opportunity kills me
To think of the time apart.
Free me from this untold fantasy;
Console my heart, and feed my soul.
Make Me Whole Again!

LOVE SONG

An undesirable devotion;
That I can't seem to devour,
Quickens every beat of my heart.
The love that you give
Caresses my soul ever so gently,
As the voice of a sweet & beautiful angel,
Tell me to stay awhile
"Why not forever?"
When ecstasy is calling my name
Softly in the moonlight,
Waiting for eternity to appear;
With its charm of everlastin' love.
Listen to the beat in my heart
Dance to my music in my soul,
Hold my close to feel the rhythm
Of my love song that plays only for you.

TWO SOULS

I met you long time ago,
Never even thinking that you
Would be mine someday
I began to be someone
That I didn't even know
As well, started believing
That you were the one for me
First day, we made love
Our souls combined like sugar & spice
We became mates and I fell
So deep in love with your mind;
Your spiritual touch dissolves the passion
That you see in my eyes.
Your love frames my every purpose of living
From day to day, I feel you near and I exhale
Whenever you enter the room,
The door of my heart is painted
With your name carved in deeply,
Touching my soul as yours
Combines to make one.

FORBIDDEN LOVE

Constant lust over you,
Something magnetic
Got me in a Jonz
I can't break lose for sh...
I like what you do to me
"You do it, so well!
I know it's not right
But couldn't it be?
That we would never know
I wish there was a solution
To all life uncertainties
I want to be with you
Wouldn't even mind tworkin'
Again, for old time sake
Let me free forbidden love!

WHOA!

Like clockwork I think of me & you;
Doing the things we do.
It's amazing, how a love could be so seductive
Would trade any experience for ours
The way two hearts devour.
Oh, trust and believe
your love making is like no other.
Hard to be with another,
only to constantly tell myself
"Lonely I am not,"
Why?
Can't find that feeling that connection,
That chemistry that makes my soul
Sing a heavenly song in emotional
Bliss you leave me speechless; laying in misery.
Needin' you here with me.
Stop repeating history over & over
Tried to go on to better & higher heights
But your love is so magnetic
That love couldn't deter from itself
Can't find the logic of this!
Only to find love again
And when I do,
I will run like "WHOA"
Cause it's not YOU!

TOO RELAXED

Sitting here, looking out the window
Missing you so;
Can't wait to see you
Touch, kiss, and taste you too.
We make love like everyday
In so many ways.
As I try to contain myself
You keep telling me "Yes"
With the way you walk,
Talk with your body
Language spoken;
More than once.
Don't know how to say this:
But I think I'm falling for you.
It's true and don't know what to do.
"Should I go forth or take two steps back?"
It's on you, because I'm too relaxed.

YOURS ETERNALLY

I thought I couldn't love anymore
Then you took my heart into your hands
Of warmth and cared only for me.
I knew love would find its way
Back home where it belongs.
I didn't have a clue of what form
Appearance, would it be ~a surprise~
I dreamed of a love unconditionally
Mine forever in my life, not knowing who
Was going to hold me & mold me
till my dying day
You made me whole & oh so completely
Together, we're such a magically couple
With an enchanted love for one another
~so divine~
You quickly stole my heart and claimed
My love for eternity.

HOW I FEEL

The touch of your hand just drives me crazy
When I kiss your lips sets my soul on fire
Every time I look into your eyes makes me wanna cry.
The sweet embrace of your arms wrapped around mine
Sends a warming chill throughout my body.
A musical sound to my ears to hear you say "I Love You, Baby"
No clue to when or how I fell in love with someone like you
I have no regrets that I did cause I loved every minute of it.
You took the pain away and gave me reason for loving, sharing,
And also giving to the one, I love the most.
You better not be trying to figure that one out.
Because it's you, I'm speaking of!

A WORTHLESS LOVE

*I gave you my all
And I guess it wasn't my very best
But even though, I didn't have much
I still tried to make you happy
In anyways possible.
The thanks I got only made me
Feel like a big fool in love
Giving your ass to kiss
Not admitting it's your love I miss,
But it's wouldn't matter to you
Cause you are so self-centered
That the rocks & sand will be
So jealous, you were of me
I really could've been with
Someone else that who would appreciate me more.
So don't sit there and think that I would consider
You again, cause "You" are on the past-shelf
And locked up for good,
However girl, I don't need you
Or your Worthless Love.*

HIDDEN LOVE

*Precious moments we share
Long walks down the street
On such a beautiful day
As we sit and so happen
To cuddle, holding each other
At our special meeting place
Hoping time will slow dance
Or stop for a while
So we could spend just a little more time together
Before the hours spent
To say our goodbyes even though
We never want to depart
from the only one that was made
Just for you, I wish I could say one word
To be right there beside you
At all times not missing you like I do.
To hear your every call
Answering your every question
Holding hands, telling you
how much you mean to me.
Followed by a kiss on the lips so gently
Just for you I will do
All of these… and much more
But it still won't show
How much I Love You
Cause Girl, you are my everything.*

HEART FOR ONE

All I tend to do is think about you
Night & Day needing to say
I love you Baby, Just for the hell of it
Meaning it from the bottom of my heart
And my soul is never content, not till I'm in your arms
Once more, only to look into your eyes of glooming sparks;
Just to gaze for a few minutes, apart I can't stand to be without you, my love.
Happiness & Joy is what you bring;
Makes me slightly bashful with the quickness,
As you hold me so tight, I think about those dreams of yours.
Are now mine and together we are and may forever be.
As one till our time is well done,
No need to worry 'cause my heart beats only for you.

EMPTINESS

Leave me heartless
All my soul disappearin'
Mind slowly slippin'
Nothing but empty flesh
Awaiting for daybreak
To come & take the darkness of my soul
And the unwanted stress
Of being without your love.
Kills me to the core;
You had to go so soon
Re-minority is there to save me
But you gave me every reason
To live & cherish life
With lots of love
Growing deep in my heart
Don't go and pass down
Every happy moment in my life
And leave me behind
Empty, for life's eternity.

WARRANTY

So content when I'm with you
As well as apart from the competition
Of both our lives;
My heart & soul you mend
With the love you send
Expressed via hmail
The way you feel about me
Makes me run in a corner
To overflow with joy & happiness
That I have finally found
Someone special to love & care for
Until my heart's satisfied.
Take it under your wings of comfort,
And caress & keep me till there's no more.

LIFE UNWANTED

The decisions of life are so hard to make
Why do they make you feel so confident?
In love, no but love takes a serious hold
Oh your decision of right or wrong
The love captured by one
Can't be profound in another
Why love when love disappears in time fades
Away your heart goes when home won't let it go.
My family & friends always told me
not to settle for less
But if less is more than nothing,
Good enough for the time belong.
What to do with the time and emotions?
Deal with them, but how?

WHAT IS THIS?

Tired of distortion
Sick of the confusion
Is this right or wrong?
We both know our love's strong
Saying "I love you"!
In ways we're not supposed to
Found this bonded chemistry in no one else.
Could this only be me?
Feeling this way it is crying shame.
Although, fortune & fame
Is not what I want
Precious memories left to hunt
Me without you in my life forever
Empty souls, never
Happy to the fullest degree
Is how to see it, ya' feel me
Thru the words I am speaking.
Listen, I found what I've seeking
For all these years
But to sit there and tell me:
I'll have to drown in my tears
It's not the way to live baby
Will u ever be mine?
Yes, no, or maybe so!
My hearts beating,
Mind swallowing thoughts only for you.
"Is this so, will I ever know?"
Huh, will I?

GOODBYE, MY LOVE

My lonely nights;
I find myself lying in a bed of salt water.
Heart-aching,
while my soul sinks in the sorrow of love.
I toss and turn to find salvation of the situation;
And yet I still see your face.
Feel your touch upon my skin
Thinking how could love end
When it just retires in the next.
You took my love and crumbled it
Into one last word, hug, kiss
Forever in my memories that you once loved.
To find another, NO, NEVER! Or WILL I?
Who knows what tomorrow may bring,
I ask the Lord for the strength
To press through the sinful journey.
So I raise my hands, say my final goodbyes
And continue to fight my love.

MIND

AND

BODY

WHAT AM I TO DO?

"Do I love her?"
I think I do.
She, the girl of my dream
I'm gon' make her my wife!
"Damn, I do love her!"
Can't live without her.
Is love supposed to be like this?
I feel so in love;
What am I to do with this feeling?
Throw it all away,
Or live with it for the rest of my life.

IN RANDOM THOUGHT

I can't go, why?
Because my heart would be sore couldn't love
anymore.
I can't go, why?
Because I wouldn't live with my decision forever
And my mind relapses on the many mishaps we've
had.
I can't go, why?
There's something about you
that my soul loves so much.
I can't go, why?
Because I would miss you daily
And wish you were here with me.
I can't go, why?
My stomach would be empty for eternity.
I can't go, why?
I think we were meant to be!
But why?

DOUBLE or NOTHING

Overjoyed at the thought of you as my lover,
I've actually wondered
What would it be like
Without you in my life.
Yes, I may have stray a little
And constantly betrayed
But surely I've realized that
You are the best I've ever had.
It frightens me so.
On something so fragile & sweet
Must I say, "I love you a million times"
To let the people see
How much you mean to me
I thank God for the opportunity
To know what real love is
You gave it continuously,
That why I hope & pray
You'll get it back in double.

ULTIMATE DESIRE

After all this time…
Suddenly it happened
In the wee-hours.
One morning, I believe
It was a Wednesday
An August morning to be exact.
We danced in each other's heads,
Thinking and hoping
To experience that magic touch
Of one's constant dream.
Ever since that first night
Temptations arisen more than once
Powerful results were assured…
The impact of lust & love
All in one;
How could this be?
My best friend & me.
Stars twinkling in her eye;
"Why?"
Satan weakens the mind
Proceeds to conquer
Our hormones…
Yea, two hot & steamy ways to approach
The Ultimate Desire.

"FAQS"
(Five Questions & Answers)

"Who are we?"
Two clones that met long time ago
Got to know each other;
Very well became best of friends
Looking for the same in one.

"How did we get here?"
Sharing the most darkest secrets
Touching and Lusting;
Each other's body, soft and supple
Wishing on ecstasy's star of love.

'What is this?'
Deep stimulations within the mind
Long lasting vibrations thru to soul;
Gentle acceleration beneath the skin
Sweet sensations inside the bones.

"Where are we now?"
Emotional bliss in the sky
Confused on the next step;
Left or Right, do we go?
To the Playgrounds of Lovers.

"When did this occur?"
Almost every time the moon jukes
In the morning misty hours;
The winds blew south
Smiling at the trees in motion.

"Why?
Temptation was bound to shake the Anticipation.

THE SIGNIFICANCE OF YOU

*One look and I fell
Fell in love with you
And I knew you'll love me like no other.
Once touch and I felt
Felt this feeling I just couldn't hide
From not even myself.
One kiss and I was trapped
Trapped in chemistry at one lock
Of a quick passionate action.
One taste and I was hooked
Hooked on the bait
Of your heart and soul.
So I explored the sea of your mine
One day and I believed
Believed that we'll join in happiness forever.*

VICIOUS LADY

Your touch massages my sexual being
The sensual feeling of you tasting my skin
Leaves me in mental bliss
As your tongue runs down my spine
My dreams came to a reality.
Your kiss intersects
with the rhythm of my thoughts
I want to make love all night long, starting with
Your feet and work my way up
Side down, you take me around and around
Driving me crazy
With your sexy ways to show that you're
My Vicious Lady.

HYPOTHETICALLY SPEAKING

*Hypothetically, you're not mine
But I would like to have your time.
To show you what you mean to me,
In ways that you can't see.
I asked you the question,
And you paid me no attention.
Why can't you recognize that I want you?
When it's clear and so true.
This isn't a long & never-ending story,
Just a desire waiting for what's contrary.
Of the substance in my head;
Made me think hard about what was said.
Could you really be mine?
Or just a dream that shines.
Take my hand and enjoy the ride,
Because this love will never hide.*

DEEP THOUGHTS

"What is this you got me under?"
I can't breathe, think, and sleep
Nor eat without you.
Some intuition of life's ending.
"What is this you got me under?"
I feel happy, sad, confused
Even aroused all at once.
Some reassurance of never ending.
"What is this you got me under?"
I find it hard to want, need, think of
Another love's truly for me.
Some funny business, isn't it?
"What is this you got me under?"
I thought this would never be
However, you proved me wrong
Sometimes, right?
"So what is this you got me under?"

REMEMBERING U

Unpurified love, I feel for you and I touch the sky
Blues is what I sing at the thought of you;
Wanting to see the end amount to eternity.
Missing kissing your lips,
holding you in the darkest hours
Needing to spend with you lost in my world.
I remember, a bliss of passion and affection
That was given to me regret loving you, liking you
Missing you, needing you, meeting you

Secondly, I regret losing you.

THAT WOMAN

*Such a beautiful person you are
No longer a girl;
So confident and pure,
You're the never-ending cure
My soul can't live without
Have me scream and shout
You name out till the world ends
Such pain within;
The mind of your love
Everything about you;
Made me a better person, lover; its' true
You see this diamond that you'll someday rock
Give that emotional shock
Work me to the last
Drip Drop of water from an empty glass
Die to make love to her in fluently
Hold her in the midnight hourly
What do you say baby?
Who? You. You are that woman!!!*

"WHAT HAVE YOU DONE TO ME?"

"What have you done to me?"
That I am thinking of you before I fall fast asleep.
Awaken by your voice softly spoken in my ear,
"I hear the bells so clear!"
Needing, wanting you more everyday of my walk
I feel so alive again having you here with me.
My heart is racing, can't you see?
"What have you done to me?"
At the thought of you, I'm blushing so
Therefore, I have to slow down
So you may stick around
"Could it be that I am just that lonely?"
Of even so vulnerably aware of the connection
We may have and destined to conquer all my fears
"Cry no more tears, and live in happiness
forever more!"

REALISTIC DREAM

One hot & steamy night;
With love making on the brain
There was nothing better to do
But sweat it off as we lay.
I bent over & kissed your lips
So obviously couldn't fight;
Temptation, so strong that very moment,
Really needed to express itself someway or another.
Couldn't resist your soft hands as you touched me
And took my finger into your mouth
Sent warm sensations throughout my body
Then I slowly and ever so gently
Kissed & licked in all the right places
Getting you hot and wet all at once
Making you feel good
Inside, where I want to be
To indulge in the sweet & tasty
Waters flowing from your secret fountain
Of love, with every stroke
I sign my name in BOLD
To claim my Nobel Piece Prize,
When I woke ~ n ~ realized, that it was
ALL A DREAM!

REASON 4 US

Weeks, days, months and years has past
And I still have an urge to caress your body.
Every second I think of you makes my world last.
My sun shines every time I see your smile,
It rains like every other minute
And lingers for a while.
Your love dries the storm throughout my life,
That's why I claim you to be my wife.
Because you calm my soul so heavenly
Cupid had retired at his job on that
November's day.
Back and forth, we go off and on,
"Why?" Nobody knows but HIM.
"Is this a dream of just mine or something bigger?"

NIGHTMARE

The warm embrace looks me up
In the midnight hour
With a tight grip you have, love shower
Trying to break this nightmare
of love that I'm seeming to have
From time to time, I find myself
Not able to hold & kiss the only one I love
Whenever I want to or need
the comfort of her love
My heartaches when your love isn't near
I love her so dear.
The ghosts of the past time paradise,
Given the negative advice
Trying to lead me to all
the suffering pain of the soul.
I dare not listen to the lines in the book.
Need to say that I am hanging on the hook
Of your love with a life time jacket
I got it in a bucket,
Your heart is mine forever,
But still the voices are telling me different.
Help Someone; Wake Me
From This Nightmare of Love!!!

ESCAPADE

At the touch of your hands
I travel to so many lands
As you tickle my conscience
I breathe out for evidence
When you kiss me gently,
I float on clouds so heavenly;
At the sound of your voice
You leave me no choice,
But to fall from the sky.
You see, we fit together, you and I
Found myself on a island
Missing you, playing the violin
"You send me to Hollywood"
Where you show the way things will & could
Be, on that first flight to ecstasy.
As I follow you through life's uncertainties.
We journey on, under the sunset
"that shows me that you are the one"
Wanna bet?
That takes me on an Escapade!!!

RETREAT

Your love bubbles over like a flooding pool,
A creamy substance
You taste as sweet as a peachy fruit
Covered in Sugarcane, your name
You wear so great
The smile of happiness
Aroma of your twat
Sends my senses on a therapeutical journey
Of no return, claiming
Ecstasy as my home.
I drown myself in your essence
Each time I lay next to you,
My world becomes ours.

THIRD BASE

Slide inside and play
Ball in your court of love awhile
Before I hit and run
Home to the field of water-base
Swimming thru your deepest sea
Slow stroking the mid-south hill
Climbing to the top of the line
Walking on red & white rose petals
Picked by me, your personal MVP
Having clues & hints thrown at you and open
Your alley of satisfying pleasure
Replays of my every night knockouts.

LET IT BURN

I lay here in bliss
Thinkin' about the love I miss
How sad to see we're through.
Got to do what USHER says,
"and let it burn".
Though it maybe hard to stand strong,
Each time I ride by that familiar spot
Where we first met and had that first date
Kiss, hug, sexual encounters
"Damn it was good!"
But I will get over it
And find someone better
"I know I will, because I deserve it!"
So there's nothing else for you to do,
But just let it burn!

LOVE MAKIN'

Her pussy molds me into the sunset,
And thru the morning dew.
As I stroke, she grips my back
Steady feeling three emotions all at the same;
Time to spell my name as her love came down
My rod of stimulation within fleshed tissue.
She moans so heavenly in my ear,
Sending me on a never-ending escapade.
Kisses my soul with so much anxiety;
As the sound of lovemaking retaliates
Like a liquid explosive device.

FINALLY, FAMILY

*Building a future with experience
and abandoned strength
to relax in each other's essence.
Is where I want to reside for eternity.
Make you, my destiny; my queen
Grow fluently with the love shown
Everyday in everyway.
Possible mate of completeness
You give me the reason why I'm here
With you by my side, I am never alone.
As I took yours to be mine,
It changed the horizon and I drowned…
in weakness
To be what you need me to be.
Your friend, lover, your backbone,
And her other parental image.
Providing well being of necessity
Taking charge of what's destined to be
Finally, Family.*

LET'S TALK MUSIC

Open up and let me in,
Just so I can
Hold and mold you.
Let me ride that bumpy side of yours.
Love to become one
With your lovely soul.
Test me and see
How I'll make you feel;
Beautifully Human
Like Jill Scott said.
Ooh and don't forget about Aretha's Brand New.
We'll write our own song of
Earth, Wind and Fire.
Unforgettable that's what you are,
And forever more that's how you'll see.
As Mr. Cole says in every way,
The thought of you will always stay.

JUST FOR AWHILE

Nervous actions I see
When you're with me.
Tend to shake your legs;
Bite the nails off your fingers.
"Do I turn you on, with my gingers and spices?"
My mind wonders, as we sit in silence;
Sensing that we share the same desire
Of me tasting that sweet pussy of yours.
Seeing you so much makes me want only you.
To be the one to get you
to that peek of never ending completion,
"So come on, don't have no fear"
Because I'm here, if you'll have me
Just for a little while.

KEEP DRIVING

Soft touch of your fingertips
The way you move your hips,
Makes me exhale to release this feeling
That lingers deep in my soul.
Seeing us together, gives me chills up &
Down my spine.
It's funny how we've finally gotten here
And now afraid to let them heal.
Sexy eyes, beautiful smile just drives me crazy.
Silly games we play make me want you
More and more, need to know where I stand
Show me where to go and I'll follow
You to ecstasy and never return.

THE BOMB

Your eyes penetrate my soul
Every time they meet mine.
Your arms comfort my love
Whenever you hold me;
Your kiss taps on my every emotion
As you taste my lips.
Your gentle touch moves my heart
And tell me you're the one.
"Don't change anything,
cause you are the bomb girl!"
The time we spend together is endless!
The love we make on occasions is magical!
The personal conversations we have are joyful!
The feelings we've developed are irresistible!
The future plans we share are amazing!
So baby, don't change a thing!
You are the bomb, girl!!!

TENSION

Enhance love
With a passionate kiss
Upon my luscious lips
Sets my soul on fire
Teasing my every emotion
With your touch of a Goddess,
Waiting to be called
By the only one that loves you.
Taste the sweetness
With constant strokes down below
Ride with me
On this wet rollercoaster
Of my explosive device.
Hold me tight baby,
And cum with me more than twice.

PRIVATE SALUTE

*As I watch you slumber,
I travel thru the doors of your dream world.
I see that I'm in every one of them.
Your world is no bore to me;
I could live there for days.
It's full of pleasure assured adventures
with the physical social activity.
You give me your hand and invite me
to co-write every climax shared.
I am paid with a continuing contract
that my tongue has signed.
United by the tingles at the bottom
of your g-spot gave me the official notice;
that the moans of satisfaction certifies me
as your number one lover.*

WEEKEND CHORE

Question me not about my weekend,
it shows on my lips.
I sniff the natural scent of what God gave us
to reflect on the days just left.
And it was as clean as the breeze.
Thru the trees laid the image of a dream
I've once had.
Me and my lover, you,
dancing in bed to our own beat.
Question me, how fast or how slow?
You want me to go,
deep into the middle of your fantasy place.
I welcome myself with the tip of my Mandingo;
Inclement of temperatures arises,
and your love comes down.
I clock in with a kiss,
on every inch of skin I see.
Then I take intervals of your natural sweetness,
cleaning up around my house.

NEEDIN' U

Missin' anticipation
On your love when it's not near;
Soft & sweet voice I long to hear.
"I can't believe that I feel
Like this, achin' for you to heal
The internal pain; that the genital area
Can't seem to bare to release the tension."
You make so hard to calm
Until the pleasure of an overflowin'
Tasty treasure assures me
"Satisfaction's Guaranteed!"
So stop this sexual composure of needin' you.

EXPERIENCED LUST

*Awaken by your love
Kissing me slowly
With passion, she caught me,
Lost in despair of reality
Knocking on the door.
I look to see that my love
Belongs to someone else,
But there we were living in a fantasy's world.
What we felt was real to us
And what time was lust.
For that feeling beneath it all
It was an indescribable pleasure;
That came from heaven
when two bodies intertwine.
Your sex appeals, hugs, kisses, moans, smiles,
Laughter, and tears of joy & pain,
My heart and soul cries for the inexperienced.*

A LIE

Missin' your touch,
Feelin' my soul come to life
Needin' your love
To caress my heart.
You were my everything.
"Come here to fill this void that I have"
Only you can heal.
My unwanted lust that builds up
From time to time,
I think of all the good times
Outweighing the bad.
Losin' my mind slowly goin' insane,
Only to find out that I was lovin' a lie.

INSANITY RELEASE

Something is happening
and I don't know what it is
Quick, make it stop before I lose it
Can't make up my mind
Do I stay or leave?
Fight or let go?
I don't know, just don't know.
I can't take this feeling.
Will this time be different?
Or will we escalate to higher heights?
Just like the dream of the lover's quall.
You mean so much to me
But yet, I feel like I'm losing you.
What caused this? I don't know, so don't ask.
Makes me hold me head or even pull my hair out.
Crazy about you, can't you see.
I can't give up...
On what I've had Déjà vu about since we split.
How do I get this insanity to flea from my mind?
I sit back and grasp what I love the most;
And that's you!

OVERTIME

The clock strikes;
Time is now!
I enter your castle of love,
Serving you long powerful strokes.
The heated moisture of your inner self
Greets me with a kiss.
I return the favorable feeling.
As I ask for more,
Dreams to yet come true.
Working the middle all night
Long, as you say my name
At the crack of dawn,
We gon' do it again!

CAN I???

Can I hold you hand?
And walk down lover's lane.
Can I touch your soul?
And make you exhale constantly.
Can I caress your heart?
And call you "my wife".
Can I kiss your lips?
And get you fully aroused.
Can I undress you?
And converse with your body.
Can I give you a tongue bath?
And cause much tension.
Can I play with your mind?
And tease your every thought.
Can I hear you call my name?
And make you cum more than ever.
Can I…? Can I…?
Tell me Suga, Can I?

LOVE ME COMPLETELY

Come heal the body
The body that wants you
So badly, I can't lie
Put out the burning flame
That's hidden within
"Hold me, please me, And Tease Me"
Kiss the open wound of my broken heart.
"Love Me Completely"
Leave no space for others to hinder;
Our everlastin' love that we have.
Can't stand to be apart from you, my love~
I have to have you near
My heart & soul at all times
Although, this may seem impossible
So just do you best to Love Me Completely!

AN EXPLOSIVE WITHIN

Every time I look into your eyes
A feeling comes over me;
Just like the earth is surrounded by our love.
Beautiful colors of the rainbow,
I see your deepest thoughts.
The touch of your hand
Electric vibrant chills go through my body
Little things you say and do
Sends me on a heavenly ride ~~boo~~
When I kiss your lips ~~so soft & supple~~
I sit on a high loft and
heav'n door swings open
An Angel smiles & sings a song of love eternally
I feel her lava is hot & steamy
Streaming down the valley of
happy matrimony glooming,
Bomb blasting my heart with your Explosive Love.

SURRENDER TO LOVE

Mood taken moments stir my heart,
Deep acceleration to the mountain of love
Smooth absorbent substance flowin'
Like an explosion of emotional aide.
Abundantly lovin' you ablaze.
Every time you are near
My tongue sings a song of lock ~n~ key
To love, under your safety
Locked up for good ~ unleashed ~
Never again, your love is my love
Can't take not having you here
With me, to hold, kiss, and taste.
Whenever I feel the need
So as soon as the time cums;
I am going to bow down
Cause with you,
I will abide forever more.

LOVE DOCTOR

I caress your heart with my warm embrace
Touchin' your soul with a soft passionate kiss
I tease your every emotion with my
muscle of speech
Lickin' the deepest valley in the south
Supplying you with such physical attractions,
Quick reactions, steady contraction
within your thighs
At the gentle touch of my tongue
Diagnosing you with my love-making virus
Only I can cure that constant pain
So let the love doctor take charge
While your soul calls out my name
And ask for more
Of the Doctor's Medicine!

THE JOY YOU BRING

Remembering you so well
That very moment I fell
So deep in love, with such precious jewel
You are a beautiful individual
I have to thank the sweet Lord above
For sending me you & your enchanted love.
Making love is an everyday thing
You make me forever sing
About the happiness that you bring
Into my life,
Every time I lay my eyes upon your lovely face:
Lead me to long for
Your love, I've sunk into with my teeth
I take a bite
As my taste buds taps your name
in a love-dance.
Whenever I get a chance
I love you with my whole heart
Right from the start,
Jr. High School was the place
We met, surprising me when I saw your face
You have no clue of the Joy You Bring!

DEEP INSIDE

Look into my soul
Search my heart;
There's you will see
What you really mean to me.
Together is what we'll be
Forever and a day
Can't wait to say "I DO",
How I love you more
With every breath that I take.
Every move I make
To get closer to you;
Is what I'm pondering on
Every minute of the hour.
I wish there was a spell or potion
That I knew to arrive
Whenever & wherever I please
Just to look into your eyes.
Can't leave without holding you in my arms,
just to see you smile of such happiness,
Showing me that I am the one
You want to be with for eternity.

FIRST NIGHT

Shy and sexy at the same time
Thinkin' & wantin' to pursue on
"Gettin' the skins" as they say; Why not?
Opportunity's staring at you
Face to face & eye to eye
Scared of making the wrong moves
Dying to taste the warm waters
Flowing so slowly
Asking myself what to do next;
Couldn't look you in the face
And talk to you not once
To bashful to tell you
Just what I wanted that moment
Confession without moving a lip
Helped to pass time away
Wondering what you are like;
Or if you are going to make an attempt;
To have you on our first night.

IN THE HEAT OF THE MOMENT

Her pussy greets me with open hinges
As I enter with smooth and wet kisses,
Like fireworks as the heat rises.
The means of you devouring my sweet rod
With every inch, has me speechless
Givin' it to me more with every stroke.
The feeling of you creamin' over what's yours
Intrigues me for another hour
Increasing energy with every moan
Of satisfied pleasure that I give
My baby for life,
I love the love we make
Because its you that I love
So dear are to me
Want you to stay with me.
As I soak in my tears,
The horizon of romance appears.

ADDICTIVE

*One kiss of your lips
The waters begins to flow
Like a river, never ending
Satisfaction, arousing
Thru my body at the touch
Of your tongue below the belt
Such electricity traveling
From my head to toe
No one has ever made me
Feel like the world is on my shoulders
When we make love full of expressions
From your motion in the ocean
Gives me the greatest feeling;
Words could never explain
Just the thought of it
Makes me yearn for more
I wonder about me being hooked;
And this maybe true
But let's just say your love is Addictive!*

SEXUAL HEALING

Let me insert you with my love,
Make your walls scream my name.
Play drums on the door of your house of affection
And passion flowin' valley,
Let me overrule you as I make love to your mind;
While I give your soul
Constant lip-music of heat burning up inside.
Let me hear those deep confessions as you moan
Whisperin' softly in my ear
Let me give you the Sexual Healing
That you could never dream of.

WET DREAM

*I wanna slip and slide
Inside and ride the waves
of your river that was made
Only by me your lover.
Let me cover you with my essence
And make you whole.
I wanna dip my tongue of magic
Into that melted butter substance
That you marinade for me.
I wanna let you ride
My Tower of Pleasure,
'Cause its open after midnight.
I give you sight of that wonderful
Moment of outstanding climax;
With the understanding that I am who I am.
Let me be that someone to get you there
When I am not there.
I wanna think about the way you say
"OOH BABY,"
And get wet in the shower of your love;
To only wake up in a cold sweat!*

A FIEND'S THOUGHT

Deep penetration,
Sweet temptation, quick ambition
Let's not forget sexual tension;
Your love is so addictive.
I just got to have it open ~exclusively~
247 is my time-span
To get some on every hand
Like drugs, you got me hooked
See girl, even shocked
Incredibly speechless
To the power of heartless
Mind, body, more soul
Such an everlasting hold
You got me,
Now tell me; do I have you?
If not, can I?

SO ANXIOUS

*So anxious to take you
in my arms and never let go.
So anxious to kiss those lips
and taste your love.
So anxious to awake
with you by my side.
So anxious to hear you
Scream my name all night.
So anxious to say "I Do"
and become your wife forever.
So anxious to just make you
the happiest woman in the world.
So anxious to see your lovely face
smiling at me once more.
So anxious to have & to hold you
till we both depart from earth.*

INCREDIBLE

Your voice sends me to a wondrous stance
It makes me quiver in a cold sweat.
Your eyes stab my every motion of living.
It quickens my heartbeat with passion.
Your hand plays a significant role
with its gentle touch.
It moves me to another human resource.
Your kiss sets a permanent smile
upon the door of my soul.
It greets me with an unforgettable appeal.
Your smile gives me a spontaneous feeling
within my vessels.
It shows me a bundle of happiness for a lifetime.
Your laugh lets me know that you're sincerely
enjoying my company.
It makes me join you to feel your expression.
Your lovemaking is so exquisite deep down
within my soul.
It brings tears to my eyes at the mere thought.
You are just that incredible!

THE LOVE WE'VE MADE

As I lay waiting for her
Entry to my private room
My mind escalates to what I assume
It's going to be, wonderful love of a cloud
Floating on anticipation of ecstasy.
Submerging together to the tone
That was playing in our heads.
My rod filled her secret place
And I mastered it to the tee,
Causing multi-orgasms to flow.
When she joins the horizon
And entered my world.
We made the sun come down
Then heaven smiled at us
While the rain pours,
We embrace the beauty of the love we've made!

MORE & MORE

Even though I have someone else in my life,
I still miss her gentle touch and tender kiss.
I hunger for that love between the sheets;
But I am trying to disregard her.
Still I can't resist her love
I tried to turn my back away from her.
But she knew just what to do to
Turn me around
Just because she knows me when it comes to love,
That doesn't mean I am gonna go along with her,
I found myself thirsting for More & More.

AT ARRIVAL

Gazing into the sunset
I see a reflection of you,
As the water roll
Mine eyes glare at your soul;
And I listen to hear the roar
From down under as you
Disappear in the night.
Leaving me to wonder
Will I see you again?
"Yes, in my dreams,"
There you will be
Waiting for me to appear.
To join the love that you
Have to give me; everyday
And every night at arrival.

Mixed Feelings vs. Heavy Questions

How do you leave one and run to the other?
When you held one's child close to your heart.
But you and the other are completely in love.
Also planning a life together with kids of your own.
How do you just say no when your heart says yes?
When one ask you to be there when she needs you.
But the other has a problem with it.
Also, thinks that your new relationship is in a stake.
How do you just through everything out the window?
To build a new life with the other.
Make her your wife and the mother of your child.
Also, when she is everything that I have ever asked for.
How do you just ignore what your heart still holds?
When your soul is now completed with the other.
But one can't seem to get the point that you have moved on.
Also, when you don't re-act the same whenever she calls or touches you.
How do you just act like you never cared to save what you have?
When its not in my power or way of living.
But it still eats at my mind that I will someday lose the love of my life.
Also, be lonely for the rest of my days.
How do you? Please…rescue me and set me free.

MY LIFE & EARTH

You are my sunshine
On a cloudy day.
You are my light
In the darkest valley.
You are my dream come true
Giving my imagination a run for the money.
You are my everything:
Heart, mind, soul and all.
You are the air that I breathe
Every breath gets sweeter than before.
You are my star
Twinkling through the night.
You are my moon
Juking over Vonne's world.
You are my life companion
Forever friend we shall be
You are my love
My heart welcomes with open wings.

CAN'T LET GO

Times that we spend together;
just lingers in my head.
Wanting to see you more and more
I sit-n-reminisce about you,
Seems like there's nothing else to do.
Joyful tears I shed at the thought of you
Though we're so far apart and yet so close;
My heart belongs to you forever and a day.
Every time your name is spoken
"A shinning star you are"
A tight and oh so strong hold,
couldn't shake if I tried.
Without a doubt in my mind
I know that you are the one;
For me, I see hopes & dreams
Finally revealed the love of my life;
Knowing that I will be more than happy to have
you as my lawful wedded wife.
Need I say anymore?
I just can't let you go!

MY ANGEL

*My mind compels with the thought of you
Conceives every aspect of what true love really is.
Take me on a soul- stirring treasure
Hunt for that ecstasy we both long for;
Feeling no pain, hurt nor harm
When I'm with you;
Gives me a permanent ID to the secret
door of your heart
As our souls meet in mid-air
Though I love you unconditionally,
You will always be My Angel!*

NOW & FOREVER

Loving every minute of your company
Adoring your wonderful touch of sensitivity
Caressed by your arms full of affection
Wanting you more & more everyday
Needing to feel your body close to mine
Hoping that time will last longer than love
Missing the moments shared by you & I
Singing songs to express how we feel hour by hour
Writing love notes every chance I get
Wishing you were here in my arms of security
Guarded for life by my love
Continuous thoughts flowin' of how I want to be
Forever yours and now its reality.

WEAKNESS FOR YOU

*Your eyes are like an hourglass
As I gaze thru the debts of your soul
Awaiting for lives when we'll live happily
Ever after is what I long for
I know this isn't right but it's okay
Cause all that matters to me baby.
"I love you and you love me
And without your love I couldn't live;
To see another day is impossible."
When you are my every breath,
I sit & cry in misery when you're not near.
Missing your touch & passionate kiss
Just having you in my reach,
such a deep hunger within.
So I look around to see if you're there,
And my weakness has now begun.*

STAY WITH ME

The feelings I have for you
Amazes me so!
How you came into my life,
Giving me a brand-new song.
I love you so much it hurts
When I can't look into your eyes
Or just caress your body.
Lost my heart a long time ago;
I breathe because of you,
I've even lost track of my soul.
You are the meaning of my living
To say how much you love me
Makes my heart sing
True love is hard to find
Or need I say someone to love
Who can relate to you?
It's incredible, how we've never felt like this
Until the reunion of past time paradise
Never even crossed my mine
That love's unconditionally would confide in you.
So baby please, stay with me!

MY DESTINY

An emotional rush you give;
Of sensual bliss within my heart & soul
Your kiss awakes the feeling of love
Is it or isn't it?
Took me by surprise to be content
with someone else
Missing you like I do,
Bring tears to my eyes
Embrace me with the constant
Thought of the future.
Will it be or not?
Doesn't really matter?
Well, as long as we live for today
For today for the next Comfort
To comfort you are My Destiny!

THE MAGIC OF YOUR LOVE

*You got me despised and mesmerized
Hypnotized when I look into your eyes
Then you spoke, killing my search of
someone special
As the hoping & wishing dies,
It's amazing how you've captured
my heart
With one sweet & oh such passionate kiss
Your touch sends me on a soul stirring
Ride, my personal genie might I add
You are my smile when I sad
Just the thought of you makes my heart skip
A beat, missing & wanting
Your hugs and kisses to start the heat
The sparkle in your loft is trying to be
What's right in the center of my heart?
"Would you be mine, I know?"*

The spell you put on me.

RAINSTORM

While riding thinking the storm,
Longing to feel the soft touch of her hand.
Her whisper my name in my ear
I hear so clearly, drip drop
Against my window seal,
And my head falls in misery.
Can't wait to see her lovely face smiling at me
So beautiful is she;
a sexy creature found to be my destiny.
As the lightning strikes the sky,
I desperately want to embrace her.
Till the rain stops and the music ends,
You'll find the both of us covered in happiness.

I MISS YOU ROCK!

QUIET SOLITUDE

*I sit in silence
Dazing; thinking about you
"What you really mean to me?"
It's like smiles coming from heaven;
Clouds dancing in the sky
At night, I dream of all the good & bad
Times we've had & more to cum.
To say I'm in love with you is a pledge,
But to say I'm incomplete without you is a fact.
Everyday wit' you get sweeter than the day before.
The beauty of you being my wife;
It's the reality of a dream.
I sit and wonder
"How & when it'll come true,
But only time will tell."
While my heart beats your name,
I will sit in silence
Dazed, still thinking about you.*

AMAZED

Baby, it's back again!
November 13th, Our Anniversary
One, two, three, and so on
Can't believe we made it pass
Twelve months of love
First you claim it to be
Strong and long lasting
Happiness is what you give
I am just overwhelmed that it's back
I adore you so much
Cherish your daily thoughts
About our future together.
We share day to day
Hard work trying to get here
But baby just look back and say
Boo, I am so amazed we made it.

SMOOTH INDIGO

The way you kiss me
Gives such heartwarming expression
To me soul deep caressing
With your gentle touch,
You tell long lastin' emotions
Flowing through my stream of love
Makes me sing a song of ecstasy.
Playing in my head, so soft
Mind blown, so easily
When you taste the pores of erection
Between my body and soul.
You've taken me on a journey of real love
Deep within your heart
Combined with mine, ever so perfectly
Your lips send constant erosion thru my bones
Come cool me down with your smooth indigo.

FIFTH ELEMENT

A sensual feeling;
You give me whenever I hear your voice.
Give me the chance to conquer what I desire,
Deep forced by your love
Can't bare being without you for the world to
stop & stare at us.
Not to see if it's really meant to be
Yes, with you and only you
is what I see, my destiny
Waits to be captured by thoughts of you & me
Together, now we both found love
It's real: like a dove floating in heaven above
Like showers of His Love
with every beat of my heart;
Lying here thinking "can't eat, can't sleep"
Trust and believe when I say
"I Love You"
Now more than I did on yesterday;
So come on,
Soar with me to the fifth element
of love and ecstasy.

CRAZY INTENTIONS

*I never thought that it would be you
That I trip over or even stick with;
Bet this shit backfire on me!
Cause I shouldna' told you that I liked you.
"I want to be with you" was crazy
for coming out my mouth
Confessing my feelings "I love & care for"
Giving in & out the other
Places to be with you for a long time;
When I already have a wife,
It's crazy, made me sick to my stomach.
Loving your company while loving someone else.
Kissing her while being with you
Dreaming of making love to her
till it become a reality check.
Never truly wanted you, only to make her jealous.
Only to find out that it worked
And now I'm stuck in the middle of my
Crazy Intentions.*

ROBBERY

We dreamed the same dreams
Made the same choices,
We sat there at the table
With the same game plan,
Only to fall short of one's reality.
A bundle of joy that we felt in the beginning,
Pure happiness filled one's heart.
The other was just in bliss of the idea,
I only wish to be the one she comes home to;
Also vice versa for the confused one.
Although things are clear to me now,
It was just robbery from day one.

"COME BACK, I MISS YOU"

Missin' you constantly
Whenever you leave me
To go your separate way
Needin' you desperately to hold me close...
Bring tears to my eyes
When I call you & get no response
I want to be with you
Throughout the day & night...
To caress your sensitivity with my
dominant personality
I yearn for the love in you
every minute that goes by;
Which gives me life abundantly?
Baby, please come back to me
And stay for eternity.

ANGEL OF MINE

Spread your wings & comfort my soul
Take me into your safety zone,
Keep me out of harm's way.
Carry me through the hard times,
Hold me tight in the darkest hours.
Fill me with your ambition of Love
I wished upon a star for a beautiful creature
To love me completely, be real true and committed
Lucky me, He found me worthy
To send a lovely angel from heaven above;
I am more than grateful.
Cause her love is what I've been dreamin'
For o' so long, very content
and don't want anybody else
But My Angel,
Who's even more than I would ever need?

IN RETURN

On the tenth of February,
We met and was very excited
24th came around, and we were one.
Together forever was what I hoped
27th, I saw you and fell
Deeply in love with a girl
That I felt highly of.
There was problem after problem
But I still choose you
Need to say that it was too much
For you, because you thought I would
Drop you like a bad habit and move on
To someone better but I obviously &
Truly believe that you were the best
So I guess my love was too real
To be true is all I know
But I see that you couldn't accept
My love at the time given,
Neither appreciated my time &
Just treated me so bad
So now you are just a bad thought
With little experience of true
Love, because I gave it
But never received it in return.

HERE TO STAY

The sweet sensation of kissing your lips
Makes me weak to my knees I will fall
To ask you "Where have been all my life?"
I've waited for love
Now that I've found you
There's no turning back to loneliness
and neither to say
Such heartache because "baby I'm here to stay!"
Girl, I think of you constantly
You're on my mind 247 and you got me
open like 711.
I bless the day that I found you
I know the rest will flow,
Cause the true love will truly show
That we will never part.
Bonding of two hearts will fold as one.
I pray that we will be together till the end of time.
Eventually, you will see that
Baby I am here to stay!

WITH YOU

When I'm with you
It's like the world has no meaning
To me, in love are we.
It's plain to see that with you
Is all I need a wonderful feeling
It is when you are near
To have and to hold until our time is due.
Our love is so true with you I'm never blue.
Always looking for the right things to say
Things I tend to do just so happen
Brings a lovely smile upon your face;
Signals me, that you are happy as can be.
Showing you that I care is what I plan to do.
Even if I'm not right there with you,
You mean so much to me, in so many ways
Positively boo; it's with you I want to be
for eternity.

"IT'S YOU"

It's you that I adore,
Baby, with you I feel secure.
It's you that I love so dear;
Wish you 're always near.
It's you that I dream of
Each & every night, "I love & want you more.
Angel, it's you!"

It's you that I wish
As my favorite dish
It's you that will be my wife,
for the rest of my life.
It's you that I want to stay,
Hoping never to go astray;
Baby, "I love & need you.
My Angel, it's you!"

FIRST ANNIVERSARY

It's Here!
One month of Happiness;
Everlastin' joy & love.
It's so wonderful;
Oh so sweet that it keeps you
Together for many more
I know without a doubt in my mind;
That you are my dream
Come true and hopes yet to come.
A glorious feeling I tell you
It's like a shining diamond
Waiting to be presented to the love of my life.
Seems like yesterday I held your hand
In mine & first kissed your lips with such passion
Accompanied by a hug not wanting to let you go
It was like heaven smiled upon us.
Leaving you is so hard to do,
When it's true love that I'm feeling
Involved with someone as lovable as you.
It's Here!
Our first anniversary!!!

AWAKEN MASSACRE

I awake with sweat dripping
From my frontal lobe
And you're not here for me to hold.
Can this be déjà vu'?
Dreaming that I saw u with someone
Other than me
Emotionally wounded, lost with no return
Tossing and turning all night
Long drifted thoughts in & out my head
Short deep breaths taken my chest
on a training ride
Feeling that death's trying to capture
The little bit of life
You left me with to dread my heart from
The beat that was meant only for you;
So I grab hold to the image of another for revival.

IT HURTS LIKE HELL

I lay here in suffering pain;
Mind destroyed because I fell
Out of love with the one
I found to be my wife.
How did I get here?
Can't bare this feeling.
Someone wake me up
Please... my heart aches on everlastin'
Pain; and it hurts like hell.
When my soul mate is out of my life.
I'm drowning in my tears covered with yours.
Wondering...
Where did the feeling go?
The one that had me open like a 24hr store,
This is now closed for good;
How did I let it slip away from its owner?
I don't know, but this shit hurts like hell.

LOST ME FAST

Such a catastrophe you brought me
Wanting me so much
With not even a care.
A heavy load you've put on my shoulders,
Why can't you help me bare it?
Lean me a hand before I get out
Without even giving in
To this war, between you and me.
I can't fill his shoes and
Pay his dues too
I'm only one person trying to make it
By myself, and you expect me to choose
When it was you that wanted me.
I only gave me because it was all I had
But you let it all go,
At the sight of fear of losing it all.
And that's why you lost me fast.

SWEET MEMORIES

What is Love, when it's far gone?
Nothing but sweet memories that just lingers,
Hereon, like all the times.
You've spent together, just knowing
there's no other.
Conversation was special love making, so magical
You've given in your every stitch of love,
Let alone; energy to shove
Everything you've done to recycle.
Like how we made each other chuckle
At all our crazy & silly jokes;
Meeting & getting to know other folks
Just led me to love you even more
Than I have ever before.
Now tell me what is left of our love,
Nothing but sweet memories floating on the
wings of a dove.

WHAT WE HAD

*The love we've shared was long-lasting
To the time we've spent together.
Sad to see it end like this;
Only to find happiness surrounding me.
So amazingly bonded with another,
Though I will hold our memories close.
I've wondered why you were in my life
When times got rough and I wanted to leave
But yet, I'd stay because of love.
You made me feel like there's no other one.
Originally our love was something special.
Don't know what happened to it.
Did it just up and flew away?
Or did I give it to the next?
Regrets not taken,
Because it wasn't neither.
You just served your purpose.*

SPECIAL THANKS:

First and foremost, I would like honor my Lord and Savior Jesus Christ for this wonderful gift. I thank him for not leaving us comfortless and for this opportunity.

I love all the weak and strong men and women that held an important part of my life. You helped me become what I am today.
I would like to thank all those who believe in me and my dream. Those who had faith in me right from the beginning: Mrs. J and the CVS #1433 staff, Wood Terrace, Paradise NW, and those who criticized me and my work. May God bless all of you!

To My API, DEA Museum and Borders family: Jim, I want you to know I really appreciate the opportunity to work with you on my project. You've done an excellent job on my logos. I thank you so much! May you get it back in double. Lori and Cindy, thank you both for all your support. To the rest of the crew, I love you all. To Sean, Dianne, Catie, Resse, and Shanita: Thanks for everything! Shanita, you have been there to listen to all my crazy situations, Thanks for being a good friend.

To my Support Team:

Mommy, I love you very much! You are the greatest woman/mother of all. I don't show my appreciation like I should but soon enough you will see. And this is the beginning! Daddy, you will always have a special place in my heart. You were there when I needed you the most. In my eyes, you are my father in disguise. LOL! I love you man! Court, you are everything that I wanted to be when I was younger. I hope you stay focus on a better life and go after your dreams. Capture them and succeed! Like me. I love you much! And Lamb chop, I want you to do the same. To my Godparents: I love you both very much for who you are. To my fiancé: I love you so much. I am so grateful to have a friend like you. I can't wait to our day! MUAH to ALL!!!

I would be typing/writing for days so I will be short and sweet... Every aunt, uncle, cousin, brother, sister, close friends (Tye, Lisa-Lee, Toy, Nana (Are you alright Agnes? lol), Peanut, Chris C., Coco, DaVante, Lauren and TJ, Teddybeardude, Kel-Kel, Mya, Nessa, Mo and G-man, Sweetie, Kim, Rockhead, Matree, Nadia, Ashley, Robin(RIP, miss u!), Jay, Jazzy Jazz, Paradise Staff, Ashanti S., Blake, Lisa B., and etc. Anybody I missed, I'll try to get you the next time around.

Upcoming Work: *(not in this order)*

Inspirations & Dedications *is a collection of inspirational poetry for anyone, accented with some artwork and dedications to the people close to me.*
(Trust in the word and wait patiently for the answer)

Like A Boy: Life Chronicles *is a little memoir. It is filled with short stories of my life. I will take you from the beginning of my like a boy stages to this reality of knowing who I am today.*
(We all make a different journey.)

True Love and Purity *is the beginning of the new level of her poetry. If you enjoyed the first one, then you will definitely love this one.*
(Life captured feelings and daily situations)

Extravaganza *is the amazing story of two old buddies from high school that hooks up ten years later. They fall for each other while they were in relationships.*
(Fighting the fear to let go and to love again.)

In This Together *is collaborated with family and friends sharing these thoughts and feelings.*
(Drawing a mental picture and feeding your soul with more than one's creative imagination.)

Dear Sir or Madam:

I would like to thank you for your support. I want you to know how much I really appreciate you being here today. So I have enclosed an open coupon to use on any of the upcoming books or promotion that I will be offering. Thanks again and God Bless!

Nelly Dreams
C & C Publishing Co.

BOOK SIGNING (BKS1)
20% OFF

CNCPUBCO.NET
"Let me inspire you!"

WHERE YOU COME FOR
INSPIRATION

QUICK ORDER FORM

Fax orders: 202-330-5287 Send this form.

Email orders: cncpubco@gmail.com

Postal Orders:
Chanelle Flowers,
C & C Publishing Co.
116 T Street NE #404
Washington, DC USA 20002

Please send the following books, disks or items. I understand that I may return any of them for a full refund ---for any reason, no questions asked.

_____
_____

Please send more FREE information on:
__ Books __ Mailing Lists

Name: _____

Address: _____

City: _____ State: _____

Zip: _____ Telephone: _____

Email address: _____

Sales tax: Please add 5% for products.
Shipping by air: $4.05 for first book or disk and $2.00 for each additional product.
International: Please fax orders and request shipping prices.

***Payment information will be requested open receipt of this form.

www.ingramcontent.com/pod-product-compliance
Lightning Source LLC
Chambersburg PA
CBHW060811050426
42449CB00008B/1626